ARMORED DINOSAURS

Consulting Editor: Carl Mehling

Skyview Books
an imprint of
WINDMILL BOOKS
New York

Published in 2010 by Windmill Books, LLC
303 Park Avenue South, Suite # 1280, New York, NY 10010-3657

CREDITS:
Consulting Editor: Carl Mehling
Designer: Graham Beehag

Publisher Cataloging in Publication

Armored dinosaurs / consulting editor, Carl Mehling.
    p.   cm. – (Discovering dinosaurs)
Summary: With the help of fossil evidence this book provides physical
descriptions of twenty-two armored dinosaurs.—Contents: Emausaurus—Scelidosaurus—Tuojiangosaurus—Kentrosaurus—Stegosaurus—Dracopelta—Gastonia—Hylaeosaurus—Polacanthus—Silvisaurus—Wuerhosaurus—Minmi—Sauropelta—Pinacosaurus—Talarurus—Ankylosaurus—Nodosaurus—Saichania—Struthiosaurus—Edmontonia—Euoplocephalus—Panoplosarus.
ISBN 978-1-60754-774-7. – ISBN 978-1-60754-782-2 (pbk.)
ISBN 978-1-60754-856-0 (6-pack)
1.   Ornithischia—Juvenile literature   [1. Ornithischians
2. Dinosaurs]   I. Mehling, Carl   II. Series
567.9/15—dc22

Printed in the United States

CPSIA Compliance Information: Batch #BW10W: For further information contact Windmill Books, New York, New York at 1-866-478-0556.

3 1559 00215 1379

CONTENTS

Introduction

Imagining what our world was like in the distant past is a lot like being a detective. There were no cameras around, and there were no humans writing history books. In many cases, fossils are all that remain of animals who have been extinct for millions of years.

Fossils are the starting point that scientists use to make educated guesses about what life was like in prehistoric times. And while fossils are important, even the best fossil can't tell the whole story. If snakes were extinct, and all we had left were their bones, would anyone guess that they could snatch bats from the air in pitch-black caves? Probably not, but there is a Cuban species of snake that can do just that. Looking at a human skeleton wouldn't tell you how many friends that person had, or what their favorite color was. Likewise, fossils can give us an idea of how an animal moved and what kind of food it ate, but they can't tell us everything about an animal's behavior or what life was like for them.

Our knowledge of prehistoric life is constantly changing to fit the new evidence we have. While we may never know everything, the important thing is that we continue to learn and discover. Learning about the history of life on Earth, and trying to piece together the puzzle of the dinosaurs, can help us understand more about our past and future.

Emausaurus

• ORDER • Ornithischia • FAMILY • Incertae cedis • GENUS & SPECIES • *Emausaurus ernsti*

VITAL STATISTICS

Fossil Location	Germany
Diet	Herbivorous
Pronunciation	EE-mau-SAWR-us
Weight	500 lb (227 kg)
Length	7 ft (2 m)
Height	24 in (60 cm)
Meaning of name	"Ernst-Moritz-Arndt Universität lizard" after the university near the fossil location

FOSSIL EVIDENCE

Emausaurus is classified as an ornithiscian dinosaur of the suborder Thyreophora. This means that it had armor plates and walked on all fours. Only pieces of the armor, skeleton and skull of *Emausaurus* have been uncovered, so it is difficult to be sure of its habits. As a relative of *Scelidosaurus*, it walked on all four of its powerful limbs. Because its hind legs were longer than its front ones, it measured highest at it hips. Its leaf-shaped teeth and horned beak were perfect for nipping soft plants.

DINOSAUR

EARLY JURASSIC

Incomplete fossil evidence makes *Emausaurus* something of a mystery. Scientists are not sure whether it is an early relative of the stegosaur or simply a small stegosaur.

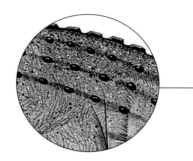

ARMOR
Rows of tough scales studded with bony scutes protected the body of *Emausaurus* from the bites of carnivorous predators.

WHERE IN THE WORLD?

Remains of ancient lava flows beneath Mecklenburg-Vorpommern in northern Germany yielded the fossil of *Emausaurus*.

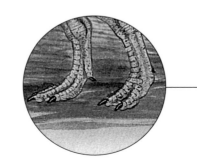

FEET
Broad feet helped to support this dinosaur's small but heavy body. They possibly also stopped it from sinking into marshy ground.

HOW BIG IS IT?

TIMELINE (millions of years ago)

540	505	438	408	360	280	248	208	146	65	1.8 to today

Scelidosaurus

• **ORDER** • Ornithischia • **FAMILY** • Incertae sedis • **GENUS & SPECIES** • *Scelidosaurus harrisonii*

VITAL STATISTICS

FOSSIL LOCATION	England, western US
DIET	Low-lying shrubs, ferns
PRONUNCIATION	SKEL-eye-doh-SAWR-us
WEIGHT	440-550 lb (200-250 kg)
LENGTH	10-13 ft (3-4 m)
HEIGHT	4-6 ft (1.2-1.8 m)
MEANING OF NAME	"Limb lizard" because of its powerful hind legs

WHERE IN THE WORLD?

The first *Scelidosaurus* fossil was discovered in 1861 in layers of limestone and shale in Dorset, England.

Scelidosaurus was an early ornithischian, a slow, armored dinosaur with powerful rear limbs that may have allowed it to rear up from its normal position on all fours to pluck foliage from plants.

HEAD
Scelidosaurus' small head, bony beak and leaf-shaped teeth were characteristic of herbivorous dinosaurs.

FOSSIL EVIDENCE

Scelidosaurus' weak jaw only moved up and down, making it hard to chew. It likely swallowed gastroliths to help break down its meals of plants. To protect itself from larger, faster predators, *Scelidosaurus* probably crouched down until its vulnerable belly was safe against the ground, leaving only its armored back and sides exposed. Horizontal rows of bony plates lined its broad body, tail and limbs. Two sets of three-pointed osteoderms behind its ears protected its head.

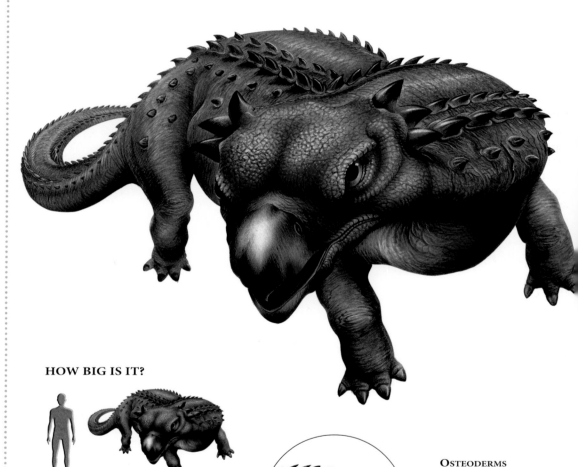

HOW BIG IS IT?

OSTEODERMS
Its body was protected by parallel rows of bony plates called osteoderms, which were hard knobs of bone under the skin that were covered with horny material.

DINOSAUR

EARLY JURASSIC

TIMELINE (millions of years ago)

540	505	438	408	360	280	248	208	146	65	1.8 to today

Tuojiangosaurus

• ORDER • Ornithischia **• FAMILY •** Stegosauridae **• GENUS & SPECIES •** *Tuojiangosaurus multispinus*

VITAL STATISTICS

FOSSIL LOCATION	China
DIET	Herbivorous
PRONUNCIATION	TOO-oh-gee-ANG-oh-SAWR-us
WEIGHT	Unknown
LENGTH	23 ft (7 m)
HEIGHT	7 ft (2 m)
MEANING OF NAME	"Tuo River lizard" in honor of the Chinese river where its fossils were first found

WHERE IN THE WORLD?

The River Tuo runs through China's Szechuan Province and empties into the Yangtze River.

The largest-known Asian stegosaur, *Tuojiangosaurus* lived in the flowering plants and subtropical forests of the Late Jurassic. The distinctive double row of plates along its spine was a typical feature of stegosaurs.

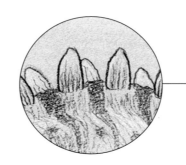

PLATES
Along the neck, back and tail of *Tuojiangosaurus* were 17 pairs of pointed, vertical plates. These made it look threatening to enemies.

FOSSIL EVIDENCE

Tuojiangosaurus' small, narrow head held a tiny brain. It probably spent most of its time cropping ferns, cycads, and other ground-level plants with its horny, toothless beak. The jaws of *Tuojiangosaurus* were lined with small, weak teeth. It shredded rather than chewed plants with its ridged, leaf-shaped cheek teeth. Its back legs were longer than its front legs, so *Tuojiangosaurus* could probably rear up on two legs to reach taller plants. A slow runner, *Tuojiangosaurus* relied on its spiked tail and plates to frighten predators.

TAIL
Two sets of sharp spikes stuck out dangerously from the end of *Tuojiangosaurus'* tail, making an effective defense against predators.

DINOSAUR

LATE JURASSIC

HOW BIG IS IT?

TIMELINE (millions of years ago)

40	505	438	408	360	280	248	208	146	65	1.8 to today

Kentrosaurus

VITAL STATISTICS

Fossil Location	Africa
Diet	Herbivorous
Pronunciation	KEN-troh-SAWR-us
Weight	880 lb (400 kg)
Length	8-16 ft (2.5-5 m)
Height	3 ft (1 m) at the hips
Meaning of name	"Spiked lizard" because of its spiked back

FOSSIL EVIDENCE

First discovered in 1909, *Kentrosaurus* is much smaller than its stegosaur cousin *Stegosaurus*, but they are alike in some ways. They share the familiar stegosaur profile of plates and spines sticking out along the back, but those of *Kentrosaurus* are smaller and it has extra spikes poking from its shoulders. It also has a spiky tail and pairs of short triangular plates on its neck and shoulders. So many bones were found at the site that it is thought the animal lived in herds—the bones are estimated to have come from about 70 dinosaurs.

DINOSAUR

LATE JURASSIC

Kentrosaurus has helped us to understand how our world was shaped, because it is closely related to *Stegosaurus*. That might not seem very important until you consider that the only specimens of *Kentrosaurus* are found in eastern Africa, while its cousin, *Stegosaurus*, is from North America. This proves that what is now Tanzania was at one time joined to North America and must have been connected to the Morrison Formation, a layer of sedimentary rocks in the western US. About 150 million years ago, both areas were part of the supercontinent Pangaea, and must have shared a similar climate in order to produce animals so alike. When the continents drifted apart, they took related fossilized remains with them.

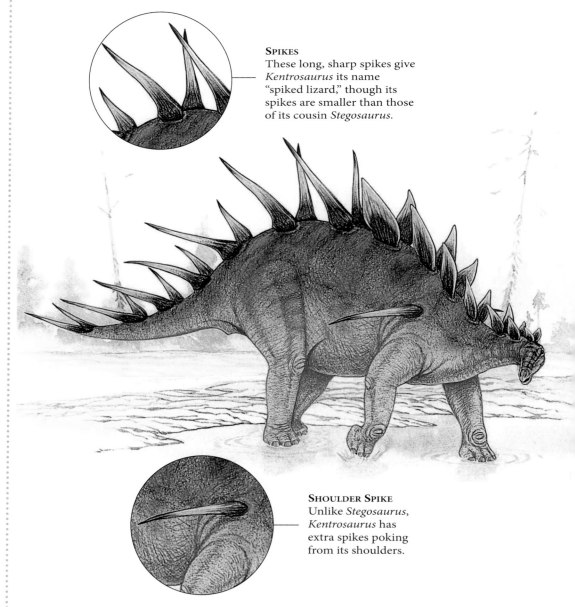

SPIKES
These long, sharp spikes give *Kentrosaurus* its name "spiked lizard," though its spikes are smaller than those of its cousin *Stegosaurus*.

SHOULDER SPIKE
Unlike *Stegosaurus*, *Kentrosaurus* has extra spikes poking from its shoulders.

HOW BIG IS IT?

GROUND FEEDER

Its low front legs allowed *Kentrosaurus* to bend low to reach plants on the ground. The plant matter was scooped up in its toothless beak. It would have spent most of its time eating just to sustain its large body.

ORDER • Ornithischia • **FAMILY** • Stegosauridae • **GENUS & SPECIES** • *Kentrosaurus aethiopicus*

POSITION OF SPIKES

Kentrosaurus gets its name from the spikes that stuck out sideways and backwards from its shoulders and above its spine. While they certainly made the herbivorous dinosaur look aggressive, their function can only be guessed at. They offered some sort of protection to the side of the body, but were not attached to the skeleton, so it is difficult to know how strong they were or their exact positioning.

WHERE IN THE WORLD?

The only remains are in Tanzania, in the area of Tendaguru.

BRAIN
The skull held a tiny brain but had highly developed olfactory bulbs, showing that *Kentrosaurus*, though probably not too smart, probably had a good sense of smell.

HIND LEGS
The long hind legs suggest the animal was able to rear up to reach higher twigs and leaves, although it spent most of its time grazing.

SPIKE DISTRIBUTION
A double row of bony plates were buried in its back, changing to sets of spikes in its rear half and down its long, stiff tail.

TIMELINE (millions of years ago)

540	505	438	408	360	280	248	208	146	65	1.8 to today

Stegosaurus

VITAL STATISTICS

FOSSIL LOCATION	US, Europe, Asia, Africa
DIET	Herbivorous
PRONUNCIATION	STEG-oh-SAWR-us
WEIGHT	6800 lb (3100 kg)
LENGTH	30 ft (9 m)
HEIGHT	9 ft (2.75 m) at the hips, total height 14 ft (4 m)
MEANING OF NAME	"Roofed lizard" because its back plates were originally thought to lie like roof tiles

FOSSIL EVIDENCE

Many *Stegosaurus* fossils have been found, mainly in the western United States, from the largest adult at 2.6 tons (2.3 tonnes) to juveniles the size of a big dog. Buried in its back were a double row of 17 bony plates. Sometimes shown in a symmetrical arrangement, it is more likely they were in an alternating pattern. So far, none of the plates that have been found are exactly alike. Some scientists think *Stegosaurus* lived alone, but others think it lived in herds.

DINOSAUR

LATE JURASSIC

Stegosaurus is a very well-known dinosaur because of the two walls of bony plates along its back that gave it a distinctive profile. It is a very interesting dinosaur because of all of its defense equipment, from the spiked tail to the armor-plated skin under its throat. This was necessary because *Stegosaurus* was a slow, heavy herbivore that needed to eat for most of the day, so it was likely to meet one of the sharp-clawed aggressive Late Jurassic predators rather often. How the back plates worked and what they were used for continues to fascinate paleontologists.

HEAD
The head was tiny compared to the body, and the sloping shape of the back suggests that the head was kept low most of the time.

STURDY LEGS
The legs were strong and ended in flat feet. *Stegosaurus* may have been able to rise up on its hind legs, balancing on its tail.

HOW BIG IS IT?

OSTEODERMS
The soft throat was protected by bony plates known as osteoderms, which may also have covered part of the side of the animal.

• ORDER • Ornithischia **• FAMILY •** Stegosauridae **• GENUS & SPECIES •** Several species within the genus *Stegosaurus*

BACK PLATES

At first, scientists thought the back plates overlapped like roof tiles. Now we know they stood vertically. They probably would not have offered much protection. The plates contain tube-like tunnels fed by blood vessels. It is possible that they served to warm or cool the blood (and thus the whole animal), and even that the plates could have changed color when filled with blood, perhaps for mating purposes.

Fossils are found in the western US and Portugal.

TAIL SPIKES

The four tail spikes were a powerful weapon. Once thought to stick up in the air, now they are believed to have sat horizontally. When the tail was swung, the spikes would have been driven into an attacker's body. An *Allosaurus* fossil with a puncture wound in its back that perfectly matches the size of Stegosaurus' tail spike supports this idea.

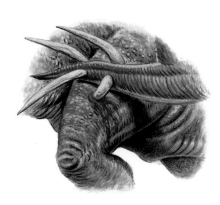

IMELINE (millions of years ago)

40	505	438	408	360	280	248	208	146	65	1.8 to today

Stegosaurus

• **ORDER** • Ornithischia • **FAMILY** • Stegosauridae • **GENUS & SPECIES** • Several species within the genus *Stegosaurus*

A GREAT NEW FIND

In January 2007, when fossils of the 150-million-year-old plated dinosaur *Stegosaurus* were discovered at Casal Novo, north of Lisbon, Portugal, they were hailed as a great new find. Scientists found a tooth and parts of the spinal column of *Stegosaurus ungulatus*, together with some leg bones. *Stegosaurus* had already been excavated in the United States in 1877, and was thought to be "native" to the New World. The remains in Portugal were the first to be found in Europe. This was not entirely surprising. During *Stegosaurus'* time, the Late Jurassic Period, North America and Europe were both part of the supercontinent Pangaea, which formed around 250 million years ago and began to break apart around 70 million years later. Geophysicists have confirmed "a very high probability" of a land corridor that joined Newfoundland, now in eastern Canada, with the Iberian landmass that now makes up Portugal and Spain. This corridor was probably temporary, slipping below the water when sea levels rose and appearing again when they went back down. In those circumstances, it would have been easy for *Stegosaurus* to cross from one future continent to the other.

Dracopelta

• **ORDER** • Ornithischia • **FAMILY** • Incertae sedis • **GENUS & SPECIES** • *Dracopelta zbyszewskii*

VITAL STATISTICS

FOSSIL LOCATION	Portugal
DIET	Herbivorous
PRONUNCIATION	Drack-oh-PELL-tah
WEIGHT	Unknown
LENGTH	7 ft (2.1 m)
HEIGHT	32 in (80 cm)
MEANING OF NAME	"Dragon shield" after its armor

Dracopelta was an early ankylosaur with five different types of armored plates. *Dracopelta* may have crouched down and gripped the ground with its claws when under attack, leaving only its armored back exposed.

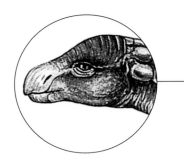

EYELIDS
Dracopelta's eyelids were supported by an internal bone. Such armored eyelids probably protected *Dracopelta's* eyes from being gouged out by attacking predators.

WHERE IN THE WORLD?

Portugal's Museu da Lourinhã houses a collection of fossils of dinosaurs discovered in the area.

FOSSIL EVIDENCE

Armored with scutes, *Dracopelta* was a tank-like creature that walked slowly along on four strong, short legs. It was not very smart or very fast, so it had to rely on its armor to survive. The vulnerable belly didn't have the spikes, knobs, scales and horn-studded plates that covered its back. When attacked, it may have pressed its stomach against the ground, clinging with its claws so it could not be flipped over. *Dracopelta's* pear-shaped head had a toothless, horny beak for cropping plants.

HOW BIG IS IT?

SCUTES
Attached to Dracopelta's skin were buried bony plates called osteoderms. These osteoderms came in many shapes such as horns, spikes or knobs.

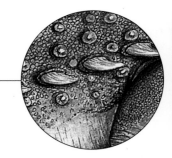

DINOSAUR

LATE JURASSIC

TIMELINE (millions of years ago)

540	505	438	408	360	280	248	208	146	65	1.8 to today

Gastonia

• **ORDER** • Ornithischia • **FAMILY** • Ankylosauridae • **GENUS & SPECIES** • *Gastonia burgei*

VITAL STATISTICS

FOSSIL LOCATION	Utah
DIET	Herbivorous
PRONUNCIATION	gas-TOE-nee-ah
WEIGHT	Unknown
LENGTH	20 ft (6 m)
HEIGHT	Unknown
MEANING OF NAME	"Gaston's" because Rob Gaston found the first specimens

WHERE IN THE WORLD?

So far, *Gastonia* is known only from the Cedar Mountain Formation in Utah. However, it is very similar to related forms from the Lower Cretaceous Period of southern England.

Take one look at *Gastonia* and it's clear that all those spikes and plates were for protection more than anything. But species recognition was another function.

SACRAL SHIELD
The upper part of Gastonia's pelvic area was protected by thick skin packed with osteoderms. These mostly tiny osteoderms fused together in life making a single bony shield.

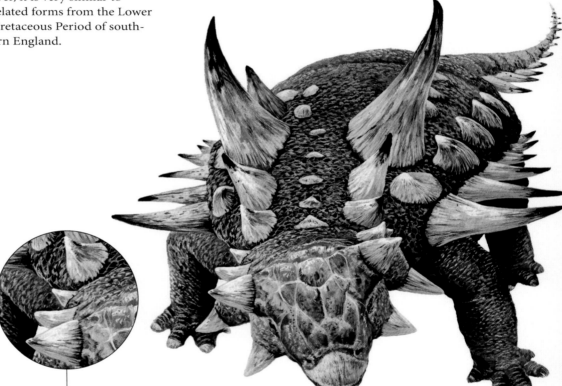

FOSSIL EVIDENCE

Gastonia, first named in 1998, is known from many different pieces of bonebed skeletal material from the Cedar Mountain Formation, which was deposited during the last half of the Early Cretaceous. Because the fossils are scattered and mixed together, it is hard to know how many osteoderms each Gastonia had, but having so many fossil pieces, its abundance makes it the most completely known polacanthine ankylosaur. It is also found with the large carnivorous dinosaur *Utahraptor* and many other dinosaurs. Even though many different types of dinosaurs are common in these deposits, the study of this very rich fauna only really began in the early 1990s.

DINOSAUR

EARLY CRETACEOUS

ARMOR
Many of the osteoderms in Gastonia's skin were very different from each other. A good understanding of their position on the body can help identify the ones found loose on the ground.

HOW BIG IS IT?

AN EFFECTIVE DETERRENT
Polacanthines are a subgroup of armored dinosaurs whose bodies were covered with spikes and plates, but whose tails did not have clubs. Instead, a dinosaur of this type had triangular, blade-like armor running down each side of its tail. This could have been used as an effective deterrent or weapon by swinging it side to side.

TIMELINE (millions of years ago)

540	505	438	408	360	280	248	208	146	65	1.8 to today

Hylaeosaurus

• **ORDER** • Ornithischia • **FAMILY** • Anklyosauridae • **GENUS & SPECIES** • *Hylaeosaurus armatus*

VITAL STATISTICS

FOSSIL LOCATION	England and possibly France
DIET	Herbivorous
PRONUNCIATION	Hi-LEE-oh-SAWR-us
WEIGHT	1 ton (1.1 tonnes)
LENGTH	10-20 ft (3-6 m)
HEIGHT	Unknown
MEANING OF NAME	"Forest lizard" named for the lower Cretaceous Wealden deposit at Tilgate Forest, Sussex, England

FOSSIL EVIDENCE

Hylaeosaurus was only the third dinosaur to be named (before the term "dinosaur" had even been created). The first fossil was discovered in 1832, and includes the front end of a skeleton without most of its head. Since then, other fossils have allowed us to conclude that it had three long spines on its shoulder, two on its hip and three rows of armor running down its back. The original fossil discovery is displayed in the Natural History Museum in London, still embedded in the limestone where it was found.

DINOSAUR

EARLY CRETACEOUS

Hylaeosaurus doesn't seem well-equipped for attack, but spines and armor meant that it was vulnerable mainly if a predator flipped it over, exposing its underbelly.

MOUTH
Hylaeosaurus used its bony beak to crop low-lying plants, and leaf-shaped cheek teeth for chopping.

Hylaeosaurus was certainly found in England, but a fossil from France may have been misidentified.

HEAD
Its head was longer than it was wide, but since the best fossil is incomplete, little more is known.

HOW BIG IS IT?

TIMELINE (millions of years ago)

540	505	438	408	360	280	248	208	146	65	1.8 to today

Polacanthus

• **ORDER** • Ornithischia • **FAMILY** • Ankylosauridae • **GENUS & SPECIES** • *Polacanthus foxii*

VITAL STATISTICS

FOSSIL LOCATION	England
DIET	Herbivorous
PRONUNCIATION	Pole-ah-CAN-thus
WEIGHT	1 ton (1.1 tonnes)
LENGTH	13 ft (4 m)
HEIGHT	Unknown
MEANING OF NAME	"Many prickles"

Polacanthus was a squat creature who walked slowly on four legs in search of food. It may have lived in herds that traveled alongside *Iguanodon*.

BODY
Horn-covered plates along the top of its body and spikes jutting from its shoulder, spine and tail protected it from predators.

WHERE IN THE WORLD?

Polacanthus was found across what is now Western Europe.

FOSSIL EVIDENCE

An incomplete skeleton of *Polacanthus*, missing its head, neck, forelimbs and anterior armor plates, was discovered on the Isle of Wight, England, in 1865. The wind and waves caused erosion, which wore away the coast and exposed the fossil. It was first thought that *Polacanthus* did not have a club at the end of its tail, but later finds have brought this into question. Very few fossils have been found, so we still don't know much about many important parts of the body, like its head.

SACRAL SHIELD
Its sacral shield, a fused sheet of bone across its hips but not attached to them, was covered with tubercles.

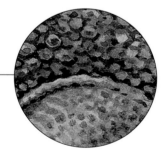

DINOSAUR

EARLY CRETACEOUS

HOW BIG IS IT?

MELINE (millions of years ago)

| 0 | 505 | 438 | 408 | 360 | 280 | 248 | 208 | 146 | 65 | 1.8 to today |

Silvisaurus

• **ORDER** • Ornithischia • **FAMILY** • Nodosauridae • **GENUS & SPECIES** • *Silvisaurus condray*

VITAL STATISTICS

FOSSIL LOCATION	United States
DIET	Herbivorous
PRONUNCIATION	SILL-vah-SAWR-us
WEIGHT	Unknown
LENGTH	8-13 ft (2.5-4 m)
HEIGHT	Unknown
MEANING OF NAME	"Forest lizard" because of its presumed forest habitat

Scientists still don't know very much about *Silvisaurus*. An early nodosaur, it had a pear-shaped head with a horny beak to snip vegetation, cheek teeth, and small, pointed teeth in its upper jaw.

BONY SPINES
It is possible that *Silvisaurus* was protected by bony spines on its shoulder and tail.

WHERE IN THE WORLD?

The only discovery has been in Kansas.

FOSSIL EVIDENCE

So far, only the skull and sacrum of *Silvisaurus* have been found. This means that guesses about its size and lifestyle are based on comparison with similar dinosaurs. With a skull 13 in (33 cm) long and 10 in (25 cm) wide, *Silvisaurus* may have been up to 13 ft (4 m) long. The fossil was discovered in the Dakota Formation, which contains layers of sedimentary rock from several geological time periods but where we have found very few dinosaur fossils. The few discoveries tend to have been found in Kansas.

HEAD
Balloon-like sinuses may have amplified sound, enabling *Silvisaurus* to generate a distinctive, echoing call.

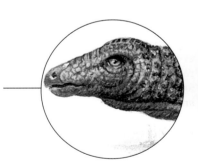

HOW BIG IS IT?

DINOSAUR

EARLY CRETACEOUS

TIMELINE (millions of years ago)

540	505	438	408	360	280	248	208	146	65	1.8 to today

Wuerhosaurus

• **ORDER** • Ornithischia • **FAMILY** • Stegosauridae • **GENUS & SPECIES** • *Wuerhosaurus homheni*

VITAL STATISTICS

FOSSIL LOCATION	China, Inner Mongolia
DIET	Herbivorous
PRONUNCIATION	Woo-AYR-hoh-SAWR-us
WEIGHT	4 tons (4.4 tonnes)
LENGTH	16-27 ft (5-8.1 m)
HEIGHT	Unknown
MEANING OF NAME	"Wuerho lizard" after the town of Wuerho, China, close to the fossil site

FOSSIL EVIDENCE

Until the discovery of *Wuerhosaurus*, it had been believed that the stegosaurs became extinct toward the end of the Jurassic period. A complete skeleton has not been found, and there is no fossil record of its hind legs. The shortness of the front limbs, however, suggests that *Wuerhosaurus* had an arched back, perhaps even more so than its relatives. Its armor plates are also unique, being small and rectangular rather than tall and triangular. For this reason, their purpose is debated.

DINOSAUR

EARLY CRETACEOUS

Shorter than other stegosaurs, *Wuerhosaurus* probably grazed on low-lying plants. With forelimbs that were notably short, and hips over 4 ft (1.2 m) wide, it may have reared up on its hind legs to reach foliage.

PLATES
Wuerhosaurus had bony rectangular plates on its back and tail, but its sides were probably unprotected.

SPIKES
At the tip of its tail, a thagomizer (an arrangement of four bony spikes) was probably a defense against predators.

HOW BIG IS IT?

WHERE IN THE WORLD?

Found in central Asia, specifically Inner Mongolia, which is in western China.

TIMELINE (millions of years ago)

40	505	438	408	360	280	248	208	146	65	1.8 to today

Minmi

VITAL STATISTICS

FOSSIL LOCATION	Australia
DIET	Herbivorous
PRONUNCIATION	MIN-mee
WEIGHT	Unknown
LENGTH	10 ft (3 m)
HEIGHT	3 ft (0.9 m)
MEANING OF NAME	"Minmi" because it was discovered near Minmi Crossing, Australia

FOSSIL EVIDENCE

Complete dinosaur fossils are extremely rare in Australia. *Minmi* is known from two good specimens, one of which is a nearly complete, articulated skeleton. There are also some fragments that may belong to this genus. The first specimen was found in 1964 in Queensland's Bungil Formation and was described in 1980. *Minmi* was an early ankylosaur and does not fit into either of the two main groups in Ankylosauria: nodosaurids and ankylosaurids. It seems to have characteristics from both groups as well as some more akin to more primitive armored dinosaurs.

DINOSAUR

EARLY CRETACEOUS

This ankylosaur's long legs and features in its back suggest it was comparatively fast for an armored dinosaur.

BODY ARMOR
A feature thought to be unique to ankylosaurs is *Minmi's* bony armor, which protected the belly as well as the back, neck and tail.

Minmi is found in Australia near Minmi Crossing in Queensland. Dinosaur fossils are very rare in Australia, but several specimens of *Minmi* are known.

GUT CONTENTS
One skeleton of *Minmi* is so well preserved it contains the remains of its last meal. These indicate that the plant pieces were probably mashed up without the benefit of gastroliths (stomach stones).

HOW BIG IS IT?

• ORDER • Ornithischia **• FAMILY •** Unnamed **• GENUS & SPECIES •** *Minmi paravertebra*

BONY PLATES

This small armored dinosaur lacked a tail club and had triangular bony armor plates projecting back from the hips. With hind limbs longer than its front limbs, *Minmi* was shaped differently than most ankylosaurs. It also had a short neck, a wide skull and a very small brain.

DID YOU KNOW?

Minmi had unique structures along its backbone called paravertebrae. The function of these features is unknown, but they may have been tendons that became bony in life.

TIMELINE (millions of years ago)

540	505	438	408	360	280	248	208	146	65	1.8 to today

Sauropelta

VITAL STATISTICS

FOSSIL LOCATION	United States
DIET	Herbivorous
PRONUNCIATION	SAWR-oh-PEL-ta
WEIGHT	3.3 tons (3 tonnes)
LENGTH	23 ft (7 m)
HEIGHT	6 ft (1.8 m)
MEANING OF NAME	"Shielded lizard" because of its horn-covered plates

FOSSIL EVIDENCE

The top of the body is covered with hard, bony plates called osteoderms. These are similar to crocodile armor. Those on the neck are long and pointed. This was common to the nodosaurid family that *Sauropelta* was part of, but it differs in that it had no tail club. It had a very long, thin tail that made up nearly half of its body length. This tail could have been made up of as many as 50 vertebrae.

DINOSAUR

EARLY CRETACEOUS

If an animal has to spend most of its time eating plants, it must have some protection from the carnivorous predators that will lurk near its food sources. Armor can be effective, but it is heavy and slows down movement, so a balance must be struck. *Sauropelta* illustrates the dilemma and the solution. It is a nodosaurid, a family of heavily-built herbivorous dinosaurs that walked on four legs and had armored plates on their skin. Under attack, they would crouch down to protect their soft underbelly. However, *Sauropelta* may have been less passive; it was equipped with large shoulder spikes.

HIND LEGS
With hind legs considerably longer than the forelimbs, *Sauropelta* may have been able to stand up, but this would expose its unprotected underside.

HOW BIG IS IT?

LEGS
The legs were longer than those of other nodosaurids, so *Sauropelta* might have been capable of a steady jog.

• **ORDER** • Ornithischia • **FAMILY** • Nodosauridae • **GENUS & SPECIES** • *Sauropelta edwardsorum*

TANK-LIKE BUILD

Sauropelta was built like a tank. The upper body was shielded by rows of bony cones that alternated with small, bony studs. Large pointed spikes stuck out of the shoulders to protect the vulnerable neck. Behind this, triangular plates lined the tail on both sides. The only way a predator could have a decent bite would have been by flipping it over onto its armored back and exposing the underbelly.

GUT

The gut was huge because tough plant matter was likely digested by fermentation, which requires a big belly and produces a lot of gas.

WHERE IN THE WORLD?

The only remains found were in Wyoming and Montana, from the middle section of the Cloverly Formation.

SKULL AND SNOUT

Viewed from above, the skull was triangular, narrowing at the snout. The roof of the skull was flat, not domed like some other nodosaurids, whose heads are also bigger. At the snout was a tough, horny beak that it used to break off low-growing plants, like ferns and horsetails.

IMELINE (millions of years ago)

0	505	438	408	360	280	248	208	146	65	1.8 to today

Pinacosaurus

• **ORDER** • Ornithischia • **FAMILY** • Ankylosauridae • **GENUS & SPECIES** • *Pinacosaurus granger*

VITAL STATISTICS

FOSSIL LOCATION	Mongolia, China
DIET	Herbivorous
PRONUNCIATION	PIN-ah-co-SAWR-us
WEIGHT	Unknown
LENGTH	18 ft (5.5 m)
HEIGHT	Unknown
MEANING OF NAME	"Plank lizard" after the small, flat armored plates on its head

Though armored, *Pinacosaurus* was lightly built. With a long skull, it had between two and five additional holes near each nostril; their purpose remains unclear. *Pinacosaurus* was probably a herbivore, though it lived in a desert region.

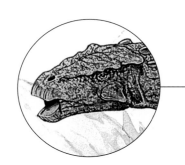

SKULL
Small bony plates protected the top of its skull. Separated in juveniles, they grew together into one sheet as *Pinacosaurus* aged.

FOSSIL EVIDENCE

Pinacosaurus is the best known of the Asian Ankylosaurs. Among the fossils found are five skulls and one almost-complete skeleton. The first specimen was discovered in the Gobi Desert, specifically the Djadochta Formation, a deposit that also provides evidence of what the environment was like at the time. With its sand dunes and few sources of fresh water, the desert region was much the same as it is today. Two groups of juveniles have been found huddled together, probably the victims of a sandstorm. These discoveries suggest that *Pinacosaurus* gathered in herds based on age group.

DINOSAUR

LATE CRETACEOUS

HOW BIG IS IT?

TAIL
At the end of its tail, a bony club somewhat like a double-edged ax dealt any predator a painful blow.

TIMELINE (millions of years ago)

540	505	438	408	360	280	248	208	146	65	1.8 to today

Talarurus

• **ORDER** • Ornithischia • **FAMILY** • Ankylosauridae • **GENUS & SPECIES** • *Talarurus plicatospineus*

VITAL STATISTICS

FOSSIL LOCATION	Mongolia
DIET	Herbivorous
PRONUNCIATION	TAL-a-RU-rus
WEIGHT	0.7-1 ton (0.8-1.1 tonnes)
LENGTH	19 ft (5.7 m)
HEIGHT	Unknown
MEANING OF NAME	"Basket tail" in reference to the wicker-like appearance of the bones in its tail

Talarurus was well protected by thick plates and hollow spines across its back and hips. However, any predator not put off by this risked a crippling blow from its tail club.

SNOUT
At the front of its snout, *Talarurus'* nostrils joined together, creating a single opening. The advantage of this is unclear.

WHERE IN THE WORLD?

Talarurus was located in Mongolia, specifically the southeastern parts of what is now the Gobi Desert.

FOSSIL EVIDENCE

Talarurus was first discovered in the 1950s and is known from at least five individual specimens, including an almost complete skeleton. It has not been given a complete description yet, but it probably roamed the fertile lands of a floodplain, like a hippopotamus, between 95 and 88 million years ago. To date it more accurately will require comparison with rocks of a similar age from another site. However, there are relatively few sites that show evidence of land-based life from the Late Cretaceous.

LEGS
This heavy ankylosaur carried itself on four short but stout limbs. Its broad feet were protected by small, hoof-like nails.

DINOSAUR

LATE CRETACEOUS

HOW BIG IS IT?

TIMELINE (millions of years ago)

540	505	438	408	360	280	248	208	146	65	1.8 to today

Ankylosaurus

VITAL STATISTICS

FOSSIL LOCATION	US, Canada, Bolivia
DIET	Herbivorous
PRONUNCIATION	an-KY-lo-SAW-rus
WEIGHT	3.9 tons (4000 kg)
LENGTH	35 ft (10.7 m)
HEIGHT	3.9 ft (1.2 m)
MEANING OF NAME	"Fused lizard" because of the many areas of fused bone in the skeleton

FOSSIL EVIDENCE

Despite its huge size and great weight, *Ankylosaurus* was likely fairly fast on its feet. It could run at a reasonable trot, to judge by the tracks of a close relative discovered in 1996 near Sucre in the Andes mountains of Bolivia. In the other locations where this dinosaur lived up to 65 million years ago, two *Ankylosaurus* skulls have been found, together with three partial skeletons. These skeletons included samples of *Ankylosaurus* armor and its club tail, which could be a damaging weapon when the dinosaur had to defend itself.

DINOSAUR

LATE CRETACEOUS

Ankylosaurus, a leathery-skinned herbivore, was huge and covered in thick, oval-shaped armor plating. Even its eyes were protected from attack by bony plates. But *Ankylosaurus* was vulnerable on its unarmored underside, so it could be injured or killed if flipped over onto its back. Despite its broad skull, *Ankylosaurus* had a tiny brain and was not one of the smartest dinosaurs.

WHERE IN THE WORLD?

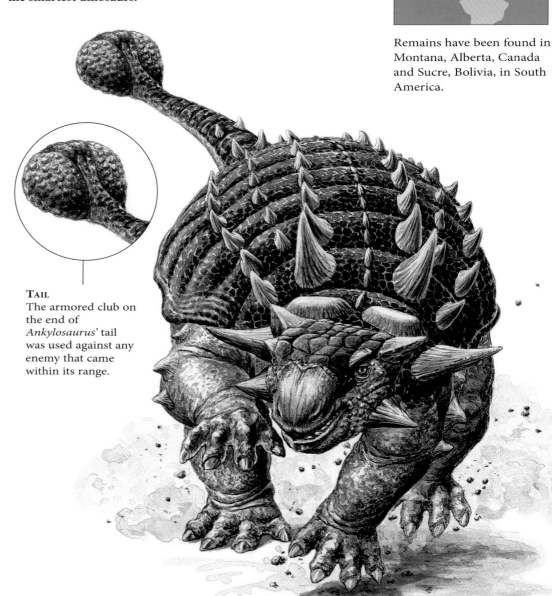

Remains have been found in Montana, Alberta, Canada and Sucre, Bolivia, in South America.

TAIL
The armored club on the end of *Ankylosaurus'* tail was used against any enemy that came within its range.

FEROCIOUS APPEARANCE

Although plant-eaters like *Ankylosaurus* were not usually as ferocious or bloodthirsty as carnivores like the dreaded *Tyrannosaurus rex*, they made a pretty terrifying sight for any other creature who might attack them. Head-on, *Ankylosaurus* bristled with long, sharp spikes and its head was surrounded by them. One shake of that spiked head could do a lot of damage.

• ORDER • Ornithischia **• FAMILY •** Ankylosauridae **• GENUS & SPECIES •** *Ankylosaurus magniventris*

TAIL CLUB

The club at the end of *Ankylosaurus'* tail was made of large osteoderms (bony scales) that formed within the skin to make it very hard. These osteoderms were attached to the last few vertebrae in *Ankylosaurus'* tail and these were supported by the last seven tail vertebrae. Scientists have discovered thick tendons that were once attached to the vertebrae; combined with the rest of the tail structure, these possibly allowed *Ankylosaurus* to exert enough force to break an attacker's bones.

SPIKES
Thick armor plating covered the topside of *Ankylosaurus*.

CLUB VICTIM

The dinosaur in the background didn't have much chance against *Ankylosaurus* unless it flipped the ankylosaur over and exposed its unprotected underside. In fact, it looks as if the dinosaur is about to receive a blow from *Ankylosaurus'* swiftly swinging tail club.

HOW BIG IS IT?

TIMELINE (millions of years ago)

540	505	438	408	360	280	248	208	146	65	1.8 to today

Ankylosaurus

• ORDER • Ornithischia **• FAMILY •** Ankylosauridae **• GENUS & SPECIES •** *Ankylosaurus magniventris*

THE DISCOVERY OF *ANKYLOSAURUS*

In 1906, a team led by Barnum Brown, the famous American fossil hunter, working at the Hell Creek Formation in Montana, discovered the top of a skull, some vertebrae, part of a shoulder girdle, some ribs and some samples of body armor. These finds looked familiar to Brown—in 1900, he had found the skeleton of a theropod (two-footed) dinosaur while excavating the Lance Formation in Wyoming. More than 75 osteoderms were also unearthed and were later matched up with the remains of the 1906 discovery. Then, in 1910, Brown was digging at the Scollard Formation in Alberta, Canada, where he found the first known ankylosaur tail club, leg bones, ribs and more armor. It seemed evident that the specimens of 1900, 1906 and 1910 came from the same dinosaur. Barnum Brown, however, did not wait for the final discovery. In 1908 he had already named the dinosaur *Ankylosaurus*. *Ankylosaurus* was not Barnum Brown's only great find. In 1902, also at Hell Creek Formation, he discovered the remains of *Tyrannosaurus rex*, one of the most famous dinosaurs of them all.

Nodosaurus

VITAL STATISTICS

FOSSIL LOCATION	North America
DIET	Herbivorous
PRONUNCIATION	No-doe-SORE-us
WEIGHT	Unknown
LENGTH	13-20 ft (4-6 m)
HEIGHT	Unknown
MEANING OF NAME	"Knob lizard" for the knobby armor on its back

Nodosaurus was one of the first armored dinosaurs to be discovered in North America. It is a herbivorous dinosaur with knobby plates that covered its skin. These plates gave the dinosaur its name.

LEGS
Short but powerful legs meant *Nodosaurus* moved very slowly.

WHERE IN THE WORLD?

Nodosaurus has been found in Wyoming and Kansas.

FOSSIL EVIDENCE

Nodosaurus was one of the first Ankylosaurs that scientists studied. No complete fossils of *Nodosaurus* have ever been discovered, which is why scientists are unsure whether this dinosaur had side spikes like other Nodosaurs. *Nodosaurus* was classified in 1989 on the basis of remains discovered in Wyoming and Kansas. It is believed that *Nodosaurus* existed in the Late Cretaceous period.

ARMOR
Nodosaurus had thick bony plates on its back which protected it against predators.

DINOSAUR

LATE CRETACEOUS

IN THE FACE OF DANGER

Some prehistoric instincts are still around today. When present-day lizards are in danger of attack, they flatten themselves on the ground. This is what *Nodosaurus* may have done, not only to protect its vulnerable underside, but also to prevent an attacker from turning its body over to get a better chance of doing the most damage. The lizard flattens itself, in part, so that its body camouflage will blend in more easily with the ground, but the principle is the same.

TIMELINE (millions of years ago)

540	505	438	408	360	280	248	208	146	65	1.8 to today

• **ORDER** • Nodosauria • **FAMILY** • Nodosauridae • **GENUS & SPECIES** • *Nodosaurus. textilis*

SPIKES
No side spikes have been found of *Nodosaurus*, but it may have had them like other nodosaurs had.

DETECTIVE WORK

Because important parts of prehistoric creatures may be missing or badly damaged when their fossils are found, scientists often have to do detective work on those remains they have been able to discover. For example, the few, incomplete *Nodosaurus* specimens were not found with side spikes common in its close relatives. But since this type of armor was so common in its group, it is likely that *Nodosaurus* also had similar protection.

HOW BIG IS IT?

TIMELINE (millions of years ago)

540	505	438	408	360	280	248	208	146	65	1.8 to today

31

Saichania

VITAL STATISTICS

FOSSIL LOCATION	Mongolia
DIET	Herbivorous
PRONUNCIATION	Sigh-COON-ee-ah
WEIGHT	3968 lb (1800 kg)
LENGTH	22 ft (6.7 m)
HEIGHT	Unknown
MEANING OF NAME	"Beautiful one" in the Mongolian language

Although not specified in the original description, the translation of *Saichania's* name ("beautiful one") likely refers to the striking preservation of the fossil skull. The find, first described in 1977, included two complete skulls. *Saichania* is a close relative of *Ankylosaurus*. It was well suited to the hot, dry climate it lived in 80 million years ago, with nasal passages that may have moisturized the dry air it breathed in from the harsh environment.

Saichania was found in Mongolia.

FOSSIL EVIDENCE

The skeleton of *Saichania* was preserved by a sandstorm that killed the dinosaur but made sure that its body remained more or less together. Erosion destroyed the rear section of *Saichania*, but further partial skeletons discovered in Mongolia have filled in the information gaps that were left. *Saichania* was very well protected by its thick armor. Ridged plates covered its body and tail. *Saichania* had a powerful club at the end of its tail, similar to that of an *Ankylosaurus*.

HEAD
The bony plates covering *Saichania's* head gave the impression that it was always snarling.

MISSING PARTS

The picture of a complete *Saichania* came from several skeletons because parts of each of them were destroyed or missing.

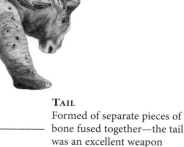

TAIL
Formed of separate pieces of bone fused together—the tail was an excellent weapon against predators.

DINOSAUR

LATE CRETACEOUS

• ORDER • Ornithischia **• FAMILY •** Ankylosauridae **• GENUS & SPECIES •** *Saichania chulsanensis*

DISCOVERIES IN THE DESERT

Saichania was found in Mongolia's Gobi Desert in 1971. Mongolia, like North America, is a rich source for dinosaur hunters.

BABY DINOSAURS
These baby dinosaurs were lucky to emerge alive from their eggs. Many dinosaur eggs never hatched because sandstorms buried them.

RICH FINDINGS

The Gobi Desert in Mongolia, where the first dinosaur find was discovered in 1922, has since proved a very rich source for paleontologists. For example, in a single week in 2006, 67 dinosaur skeletons were found at a site two days' drive from the Mongolian capital, Ulaanbaatar. The year before, 30 dinosaur fossils were found in the same area.

HOW BIG IS IT?

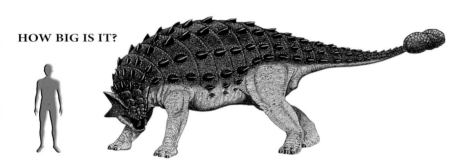

MELINE (millions of years ago)

| 0 | 505 | 438 | 408 | 360 | 280 | 248 | 208 | 146 | 65 | 1.8 to today |

33

Saichania

• **ORDER** • Ornithischia • **FAMILY** • Ankylosauridae • **GENUS & SPECIES** • *Saichania chulsanensis*

DINOSAURS IN MONGOLIA

In 1993, a team of scientists from the American Museum of Natural History found specimens that helped to explain why so many complete, articulated dinosaur fossils are found in certain areas of the Gobi Desert of Mongolia. In Ukhaa Tolgod ("Brown Hills,") southern Mongolia, it appears that, at times, huge amounts of water had soaked into the desert sands, causing massive avalanches to run down the sides of the dunes. The dinosaurs became completely buried before other animals could scavenge them or the weather could erode and destroy them. The speed of the event also accounted for the incredible state of preservation in which the dinosaurs' fossils were found. The desert sands had, of course, always been dangerous and avalanches were only one such danger. One *Saichania chulsanensis* individual was discovered well-preserved in sandstone where it had been possibly overtaken by a sandstorm and died millions of years before.

Struthiosaurus

VITAL STATISTICS

FOSSIL LOCATION	Across southern Europe
DIET	Herbivorous
PRONUNCIATION	Struth-io-SAWR-us
WEIGHT	661 lb (300 kg)
LENGTH	6.5 ft (2 m)
HEIGHT	Unknown
MEANING OF NAME	"Ostrich lizard" because of the alleged resemblance of the back of its skull to that of a bird

FOSSIL EVIDENCE

A fair amount of fossil evidence exists for *Struthiosaurus*, but paleontologists have not agreed about how to interpret it. In 1871, Emanuel Bunzel classified it as a separate order of reptiles known as Ornithocephala, meaning "bird heads." In 1915, Baron Franz von Nopsca, who worked on the Transylvanian finds, classed *Struthiosaurus* as one of the smallest armored dinosaurs with a birdlike head. But in 1994, two other paleontologists examining the *Struthiosaurus* fossils concluded that they were those of a young nodosaur, a relation of *Ankylosaurus*.

DINOSAUR

LATE CRETACEOUS

As dinosaurs go, *Struthiosaurus* was on the small side. It was, in fact, one of the smallest dinosaurs yet discovered. *Struthiosaurus* was first described in 1871 by the German paleontologist Emanuel Bunzel. Further *Struthiosaurus* finds were made in 1915 in Transylvania, in Romania, and more were uncovered in Languedoc in southern France in 2003. The strange thing about the finds in southern Europe is that all dinosaurs from this region have turned out to be dwarf species. This includes a sauropod, a hadrosaurid and an iguanodontid.

WHERE IN THE WORLD?

Struthiosaurus was found in France, Hungary, Austria and Romania.

ARMOR
Struthiosaurus had several kinds of armor on its back and tail, including large spine plates and long shoulder spines.

SKULL
Struthiosaurus acquired the curious name "ostrich lizard" because the back of its head looked like the skull of a bird.

• **ORDER** • Ornithischia • **FAMILY** • Nodosauridae •
• **GENUS & SPECIES** • Several species within the genus *Struthiosaurus*

SMALL SPECIES

Struthiosaurus was a small dinosaur that evolved on a chain of islands that would later be part of the continent of Europe. As the resources available for survival on each island were possibly limited, the dinosaurs did not evolve and grow to enormous sizes that would have needed to eat huge amounts of vegetation to survive.

LEGS
Struthiosaurus had long legs for an Ankylosaur. Its legs were not as sturdy as other Ankylosaurs because they did not have to support such a huge weight.

HOW BIG IS IT?

IMELINE (millions of years ago)

40	505	438	408	360	280	248	208	146	65	1.8 to today

Edmontonia

VITAL STATISTICS

FOSSIL LOCATION	North America
DIET	Herbivorous
PRONUNCIATION	Edmon-TONE-ee-uh
WEIGHT	1587 lb (3500 kg)
LENGTH	23 ft (7 m)
HEIGHT	6 ft (2 m)
MEANING OF NAME	Named after the Edmonton Rock Formation in Canada where it was found

FOSSIL EVIDENCE

Edmontonia was a nodosaurid ankylosaur, that is, an armored dinosaur, but it lacked a bony club on its thick tail. It was very bulky and got around on four thick legs and wide five-toed feet. Its armor consisted of a mass of plates and spikes that covered its back and tail. The fossils found in the Edmonton Formation belonged to the species *E. longiceps* . They were found 7 miles (11 km) west of the village of Morrin in central Alberta.

DINOSAUR

LATE CRETACEOUS

Edmontonia acquired its name in 1928, four years after it was discovered in the Edmonton Formation in Alberta, Canada. As a herbivore it was unlikely to have been as fierce as a carnivore, but *Edmontonia* had large, wicked-looking spikes that jutted out from its sides. These were probably used to defend *Edmontonia* territory and keep rivals away from its mate. They may also have served as protection against attack. Another self-defense strategy was probably for *Edmontonia* to crouch low to the ground so that its unarmored underside was not exposed to its enemies.

WHERE IN THE WORLD?

Edmontonia was found in Edmonton in Alberta, Canada, and in Montana, South Dakota and Texas.

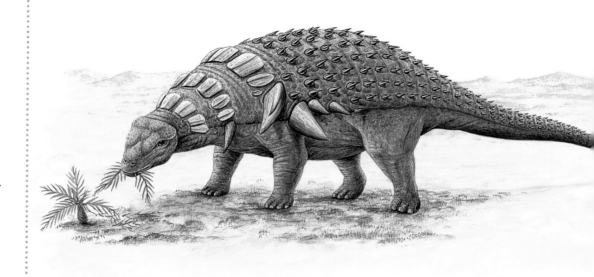

LEGS
Short, stubby legs made it easy for *Edmontonia* to reach low-lying plants, or to crouch down quickly if under attack.

SPIKY ARMOR
Edmontonia's back was thickly covered in dorsal armor, edged with intimidating spikes. The rest of its body was not as well protected.

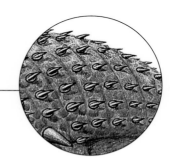

• **ORDER** • Ornithischia • **FAMILY** • Nodosauridae • **GENUS & SPECIES** • *Edmontonia rugosidens, E. longiceps*

FEEDING LOW TO THE GROUND

So many fossils of *Edmontonia* have been found that it has been relatively easy for paleontologists to reconstruct the whole dinosaur. It likely lived in the woodlands of prehistoric North America, which provided plenty for it to eat. *Edmontonia's* physique, with its short neck and stubby legs, was seemingly adapted for eating ferns, cycads and other low-lying plants.

SPIKES
Edmontonia's armor included spikes that radiated from the sides of its body, especially near its neck, the top of which was also protected by a shield of large plates.

PROCESSING PLANTS

A dinosaur's teeth can tell us a lot about the food it ate and how it was broken down and digested. *Edmontonia* had to deal with tough plants. Although it had teeth in its cheeks, these were too small and its jaw too weak to do all the work of chewing them up. Some scientists believe that this was done instead by fermentation chambers inside the body. Here, chemicals broke the plants down so that they could be digested.

HOW BIG IS IT?

TIMELINE (millions of years ago)

540	505	438	408	360	280	248	208	146	65	1.8 to today

Edmontonia

Edmontonia

This was one of the most common armoured dinosaurs in Alberta. Large and well protected, it had small teeth and weak jaws. Unlike some of its close relatives, it lacked a tail club and had spines only around its neck and shoulders.

• ORDER • Ornithischia **• FAMILY •** Nodosauridae **• GENUS & SPECIES •** *Edmontonia rugosidens, E. longiceps*

EDMONTONIA AND THE END OF THE NON-AVIAN DINOSAURS

Edmontonia, which first appeared in the Late Cretaceous Period some 76 million years ago, existed for about eight million years before the Age of the Dinosaurs ended. There are many theories about this extinction, some suggesting quick death by sudden disaster, and others favoring a slower process of extinction. One of these less dramatic, but nevertheless fatal, events seems to have occurred while *Edmontonia* was still alive. It was, of course, a herbivore that depended on a constant supply of vegetation for its diet. But evidence of a problem with its food supply has been found in rings left in the petrified wood of trees that grew in the forests in *Edmontonia's* time. These rings show that there was less rain and a rise in temperature when the extinction of the non-avian dinosaurs was close. These changes probably led to drought, the destruction of plant life and with that a shortage of food. Without water and food the last of the non-avian dinosaurs may have died of thirst and starvation. Paleontologists have discovered large numbers of ankylosaurs, like *Edmontonia*, buried in sand or mud intact with their body armor still perfectly preserved.

Euoplocephalus

VITAL STATISTICS

FOSSIL LOCATION	Canada, US
DIET	Herbivorous
PRONUNCIATION	YOU-oh-plo-SEF-ah-lus
WEIGHT	1.8-3 tons (2-3.3 tonnes)
LENGTH	20 ft (6 m)
HEIGHT	Unknown
MEANING OF NAME	"Well armored head" after the armored plates on its skull

FOSSIL EVIDENCE

Euoplocephalus has been found in several places, making it one of the most common dinosaurs found in North America. Only isolated specimens have been found, suggesting that it lived by itself, although there is fossil evidence that some of its relatives lived in herds. The armor plating running across its back offered *Euoplocephalus* good protection. It was probably vulnerable only if flipped over on its back. An analysis of dinosaur bones in Alberta, Canada, reveal no bite marks on *Euoplocephalus* or any of its armored relatives.

DINOSAUR

LATE CRETACEOUS

Its entire head and body were covered with armor that was studded with spikes, and *Euoplocephalus* even had bony shutters that slid over its eyes for protection. Horns projected from the back of its skull.

WHERE IN THE WORLD?

Euoplocephalus was found in North America, specifically Alberta, Canada and Montana.

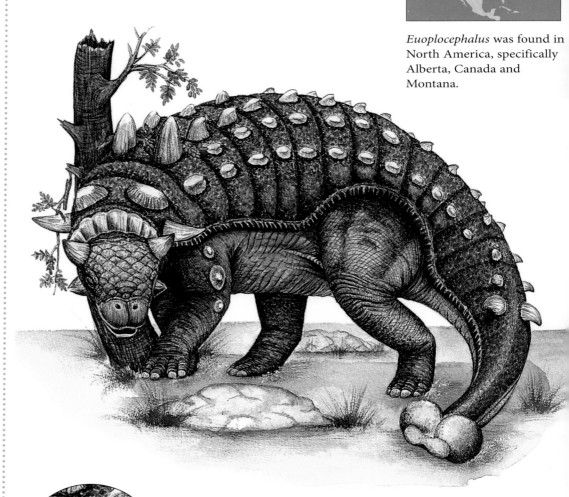

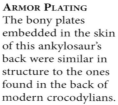

ARMOR PLATING
The bony plates embedded in the skin of this ankylosaur's back were similar in structure to the ones found in the back of modern crocodylians.

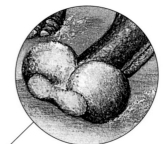

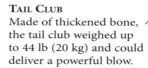

TAIL CLUB
Made of thickened bone, the tail club weighed up to 44 lb (20 kg) and could deliver a powerful blow.

• **ORDER** • Ornithischia • **FAMILY** • Ankylosauridae • **GENUS & SPECIES** • *Euoplocephalus tutus*

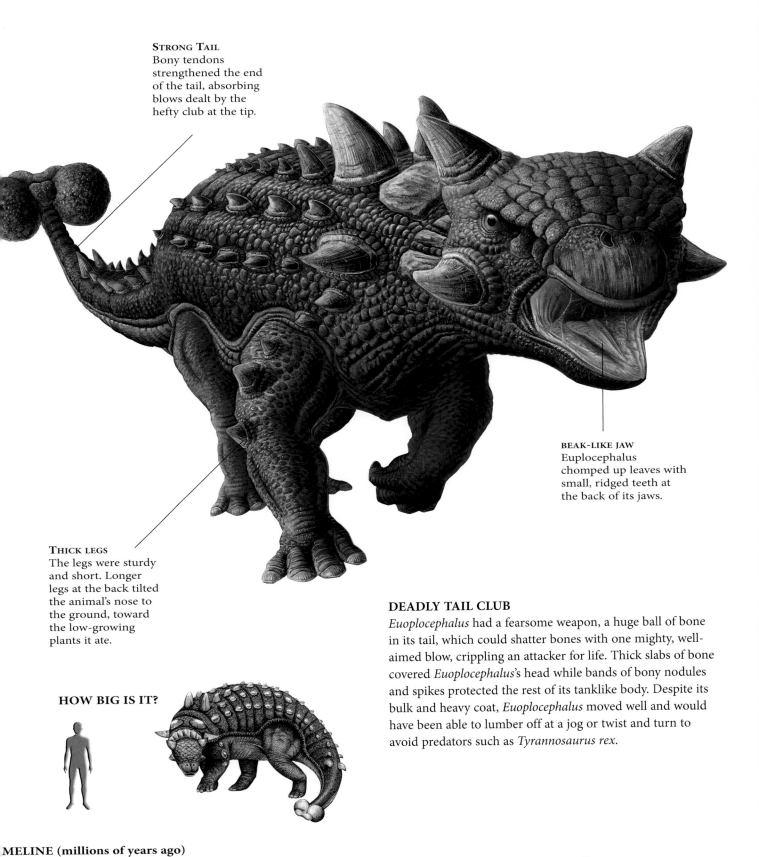

STRONG TAIL
Bony tendons strengthened the end of the tail, absorbing blows dealt by the hefty club at the tip.

BEAK-LIKE JAW
Euplocephalus chomped up leaves with small, ridged teeth at the back of its jaws.

THICK LEGS
The legs were sturdy and short. Longer legs at the back tilted the animal's nose to the ground, toward the low-growing plants it ate.

HOW BIG IS IT?

DEADLY TAIL CLUB

Euoplocephalus had a fearsome weapon, a huge ball of bone in its tail, which could shatter bones with one mighty, well-aimed blow, crippling an attacker for life. Thick slabs of bone covered *Euoplocephalus*'s head while bands of bony nodules and spikes protected the rest of its tanklike body. Despite its bulk and heavy coat, *Euoplocephalus* moved well and would have been able to lumber off at a jog or twist and turn to avoid predators such as *Tyrannosaurus rex*.

Panoplosaurus

• **ORDER** • Ornithischia • **FAMILY** • Nodosauridae • **GENUS & SPECIES** • *Panoplosaurus miru*

VITAL STATISTICS

FOSSIL LOCATION	Canada, western US
DIET	Herbivorous
PRONUNCIATION	PAN-oh-ploh-SAWR-us
WEIGHT	3.5 tons (3.9 tonnes)
LENGTH	18-23 ft (5.5-7 m)
HEIGHT	4 ft (1.2 m)
MEANING OF NAME	"Fully armored lizard" in reference to its spiky armor

Panoplosaurus doesn't seem well-equipped to fight, lacking the tail club found on other ankylosaurs. However, armor embedded in its skin and spikes on its neck, side, tail and shoulders probably scared off most predators.

HEAD
A helmet of bony plates fused to its skull, and oval plates covering its cheek, kept its head well protected.

WHERE IN THE WORLD

Panoplosaurus was located in Alberta, Canada, as well as Montana.

FOSSIL EVIDENCE

Panoplosaurus is known from two partial specimens, one of which features an almost intact skull. The skull suggests that *Panoplosaurus* had cheeks for stopping food from falling out of its mouth as it ate. In fact, so detailed is the skull that it has been used to model the skulls of other armored dinosaurs whose skulls have not been preserved. Also in the fossil record are parts of its armor, and similarities to the armor of *Edmontonia* (who also lived in North America around the same time) suggest the two were closely related.

BEAK
Weighed down by its armor, *Panoplosaurus* browsed only low-lying plants, shearing them with its toothless beak.

DINOSAUR

LATE CRETACEOUS

HOW BIG IS IT?

TIMELINE (millions of years ago)

540	505	438	408	360	280	248	208	146	65	1.8 to today

Glossary

anterior (an-TEE-ree-ur) Positioned near the front, or head, of a creature

array (uh-RAY) A group or arrangement of something

biodiversity (by-oh-dih-VER-si-tee) When an environment contains many different types of plants and animals

carnivore (KAR-nih-vor) An animal or plant that eats meat

dorsal (DOOR-sul) Positioned near or on the back of a creature

embedded (em-BED-ed) Enclosed in something

fermentation (fer-men-TAY-shun) Process by which chemical compounds, such as those in food, are broken down by bacteria or molds into simpler forms

fossil (FAH-sil) Remains or traces of an organism from the past that have been preserved, such as bones, teeth, footprints, etc.

herbivore (ER-bih-vor) An animal that eats plants

New World (NU WURLD) Usually referring to North America and South America

paleontologist (pay-lee-on-TAH-luh-jist) A scientist who studies fossils

sacrum (SAK-rum) A part of the spine connected to the pelvis

symmetrical (sih-MEH-trih-kul) When two sides are exactly the same

theropod (THIR-a-pod) A type of dinosaur with two feet and two smaller arms

Index

For More Information

Books

Gray, Susan Heinrichs. *Dinosaur Armor.* Danbury, CT: Children's Press, 2007.

Eldredge, Niles. *The Fossil Factory: A Kid's Guide to Digging Up Dinosaurs, Exploring Evolution, and Finding Fossils.* Lanham, MD: Roberts Rinehart Publishing, 2002.

Landau, Elaine. *Stegosaurus.* Danbury, CT: Children's Press, 2007.

Web Sites

To ensure the currency and safety of recommended Internet links, Windmill maintains and updates an online list of sites related to the subject of this book. To access this list of Web sites, please go to www.windmillbooks.com/weblinks and select this book's title.

For more great fiction and nonfiction, go to www.windmillbooks.com.